Print information available on the last page

Rev. date: 10/09/2015

To order additional copies of this book, contact:
Xlibris
1-888-795-4274
www.Xlibris.com
Orders@Xlibris.com

SULON
DECORATES THE
CHRISTMAS
TREE

By Donna J. Crouse

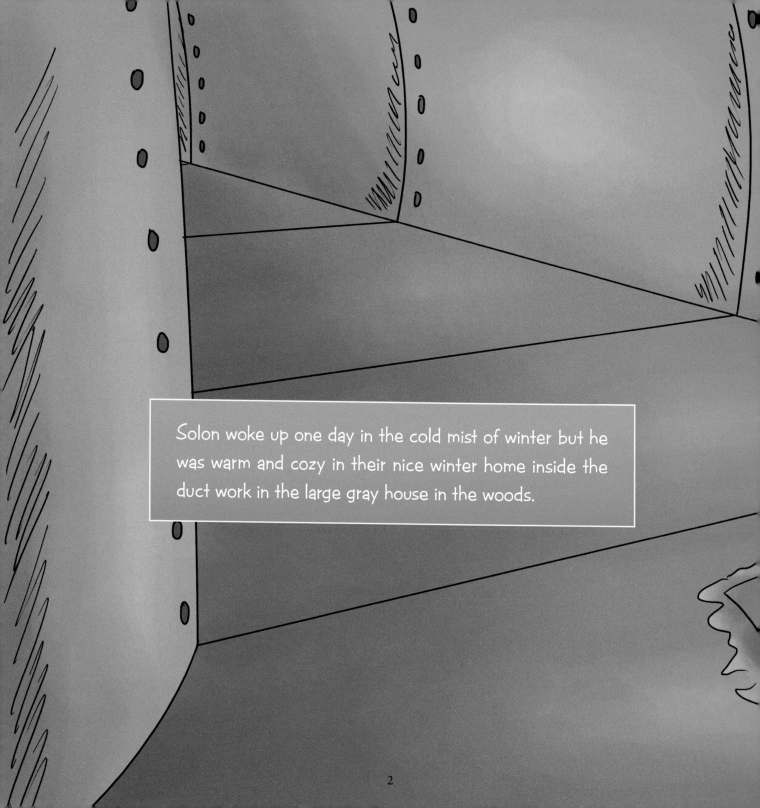

Solon woke up one day in the cold mist of winter but he was warm and cozy in their nice winter home inside the duct work in the large gray house in the woods.

SCHOOL CALENDAR

Sun	Mon	Tues	Wens	Th	Fri	Sat
1	2		4	5	6	
8	9				13	
15	16					
22	23					
29	30					

School is almost over for the holidays just three more days.

On his way home from school sulon and his friends, brothers, and sisters had been spending some time each day looking at the Christmas trees in the forest trying to decide which one to ask dad to cut down.

On the last day of school they had a big party and all the little mice were having a great time eating candy and cake and drinking punch. They were all making ornaments for their trees at home.

8

On the way home that day hanchoe who had made a trip into the woods that day came scampering out and said "Come on everyone, I think I found the perfect tree."

10

Sulon, suloo, attoo, and meechee ran to see this lovely tree. It was very nice with limbs all around everyone said "This is great, lets tell dad!"

12

All the mice children scampered back to the big grey house and in through the mouse door. They ran up to mom and told her about the great tree. Go wake up dad and tell him.

The mice children were real excited when they woke dad and he had to calm them down. They told him about the tree. He picked up his axe and said ok lets go.

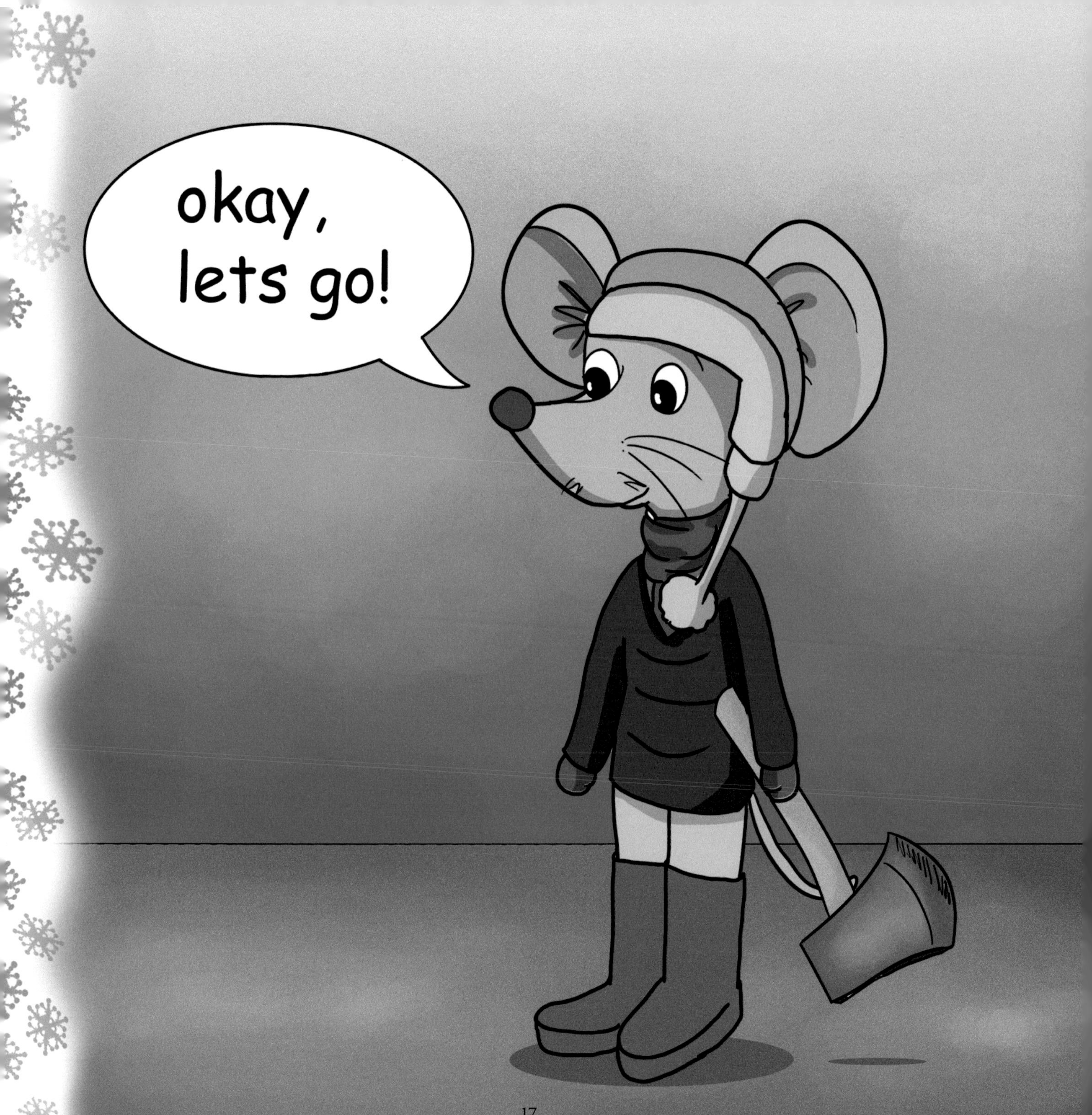
okay,
lets go!

They went to the woods where they found the tree. Dad liked it too he chopped it down and took it home and put it up.

It wasn't long before the children had decorated it from the middle to the bottom but nothing on top.

19

He picked up the Christmas balls, candy canes, and strings of popcorn and placed them near the top of the tree he also placed the shiny star on top. Everyone cheered when they plugged in the lights.

cheers!

Printed in the United States
By Bookmasters

This is the last installment of the series of Sulon. In this book you will see how our hero Sulon makes everyone happy and celebrate the season. Again it was Sulon with his tail too long that saves the day.

Donna J. Crouse was born in Fredericksburg, Virginia. She lived there until she was eighteen. She is married to Frank Crouse and now lives in King George, Virginia. She has written six books, mostly fictional children books. This, however, is not completely fictional but based on true events. There are several more books to come.

Xlibris

ISBN 978-1-5144-1572-6
51599
9 781514 415726

A 'Paws'itive Book

Dudley's

BIG Debut!!!

LJ.Bradfield